AF188393

Impressum
Verlag: BABADADA GmbH, Nedderfeld 112 , 22529 Hamburg
Geschäftsführer / Verlagsleitung: Harald Hof
Druck: Books on Demand GmbH, In de Tarpen 42, 22848 Norderstedt

Imprint
Publisher: BABADADA GmbH, Nedderfeld 112 , 22529 Hamburg, Germany
Managing Director / Publishing direction: Harald Hof
Print: Books on Demand GmbH, In de Tarpen 42, 22848 Norderstedt

# school
# lekol

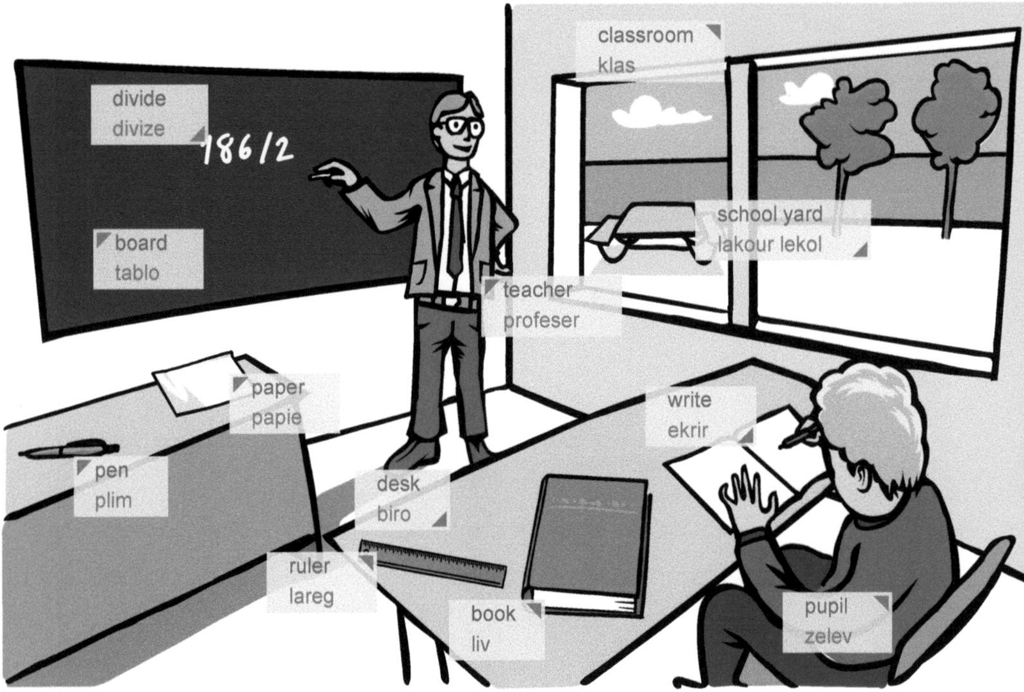

classroom
klas
divide
divize
186/2
board
tablo
school yard
lakour lekol
teacher
profeser
paper
papie
write
ekrir
pen
plim
desk
biro
ruler
lareg
book
liv
pupil
zelev


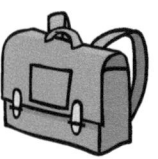

satchel
sak lekol

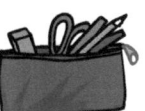

pencil case
plimie

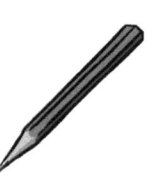

pencil
kreyon

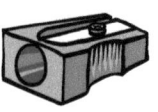

pencil sharpener
egizwar

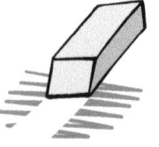

rubber
gom

drawing pad
kaye desin

drawing

desin

paintbrush

pinso

paint box

bwat lapintir

scissors

sizo

glue

lakol

exercise book

kaye devwar

homework

devwar

number

nimero

2+2

add

azoute

5-2

subtract

retire

2×2

multiply

miltipliye

calculate

kalkile

letter

let

ABCDEFG
HIJKLMN
OPQRSTU
VWXYZ

alphabet

alfabet

word

mo

text

text

read

lir

chalk

lakre

lesson

leson

register

rezis

exam

lexame

certificate

sertifika

school uniform

iniform lekol

education

ledikasion

encyclopedia

lansiklopedi

university

liniversite

microscope

mikroskop

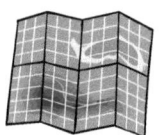

map

map

waste-paper basket

poubel

# travel

## vwayaz

hotel
lotel
Grand
hostel
loberz
ROOMS
bureau de change
biro sanz
CHANGE
car
loto


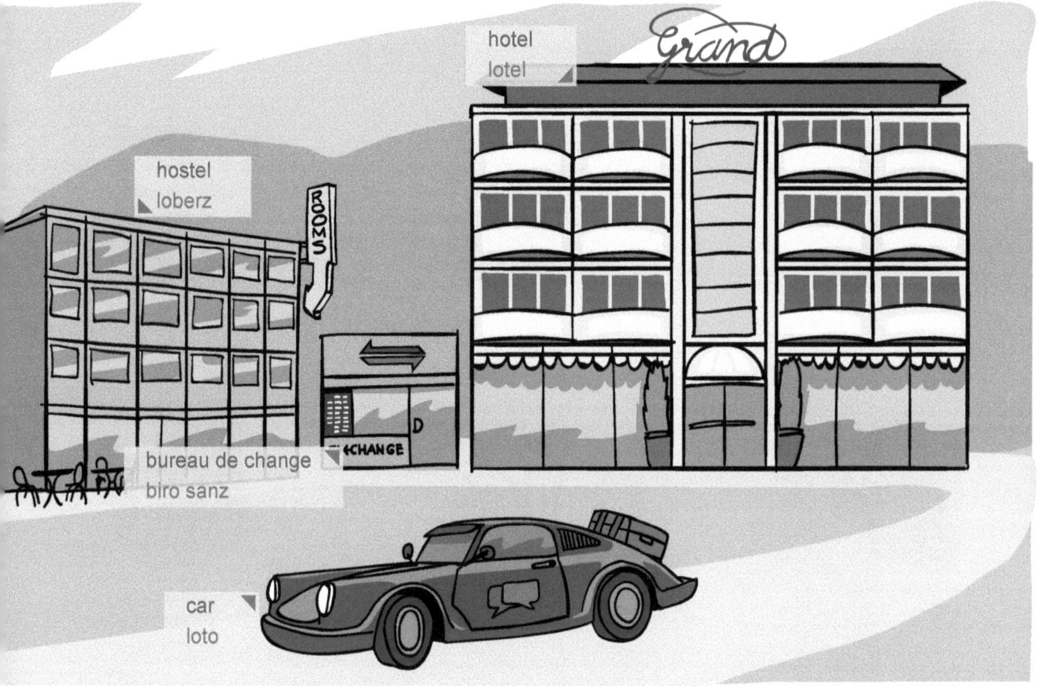

language
langaz

yes / no
wi / non

Okay
okay

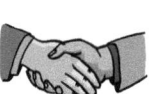

hello
Alo

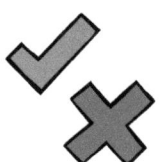

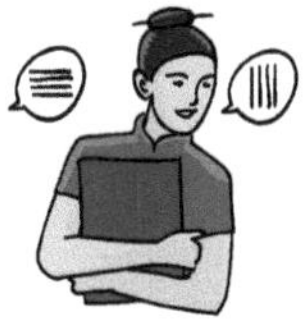

translator
tradikter

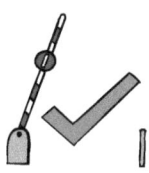

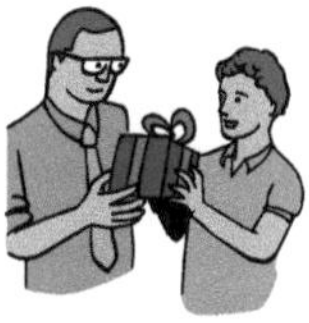

Thank you
Mersi

how much is…?

komie sa..?

I do not understand

Mo pa pe konpran

problem

problem

Good evening!

Bonswar!

Good morning!

Bonzour!

Good night!

Bonn nwi!

bye bye

o-revwar

direction

direksion

luggage

bagaz

bag

sak

backpack

sak-a-do

guest

ot

room

pies

sleeping bag

sak kousaz

tent

latant

tourist information

lofis tourism

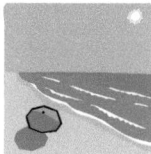

beach

laplaz

credit card

kart kredi

breakfast

ti-dezene

lunch

dezene

dinner

dine

ticket

biye

lift

lasanser

stamp

tem

border

frontier

customs

ladwann

embassy

lanbasad

visa

viza

passport

paspor

# transport
# transpor

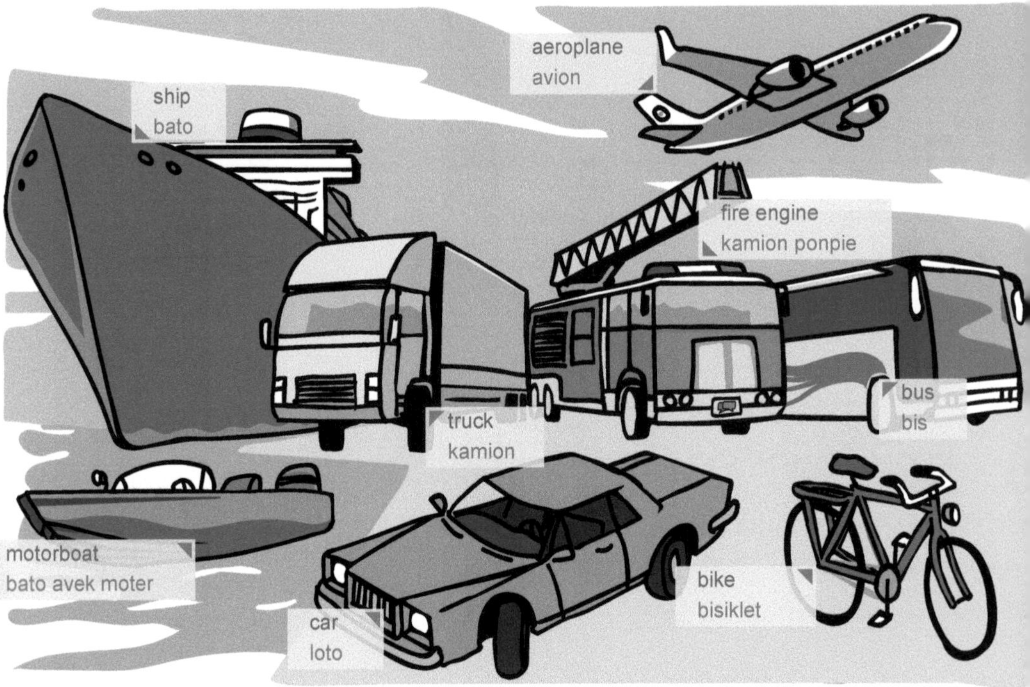

aeroplane
avion
ship
bato
fire engine
kamion ponpie
bus
bis
truck
kamion
motorboat
bato avek moter
bike
bisiklet
car
loto


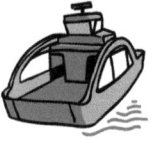

ferry
feri

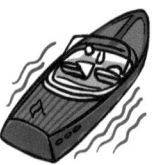

boat
bato

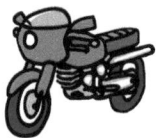

motorbike
motosiklet

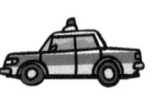

police car
loto lapolis

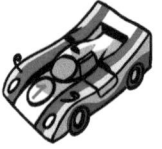

racing car
loto lekours

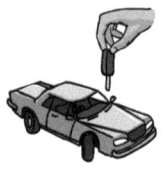

rental car
loto lokasion

car sharing

ko-vwatiraz

breakdown truck

kamion towing

refuse truck

kamion salte

motor

moter

fuel

lesans

petrol station

filing

traffic sign

pano indikasion

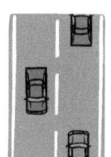

traffic

trafik

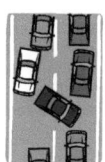

traffic jam

anbouteyaz

car park

parking

train station

stasion trin

tracks

ray

train

trin

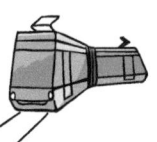

tram

tram

carriage

vagon

transport - transpor

helicopter

elikopter

airport

aeropor

tower

towing

passenger

pasaze

container

kontener

carton

karton

cart

sario

basket

panie

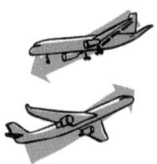

take off / land

dekole / aterir

## city

## lavil

village

vilaz

city centre

sant-vil

house

lakaz

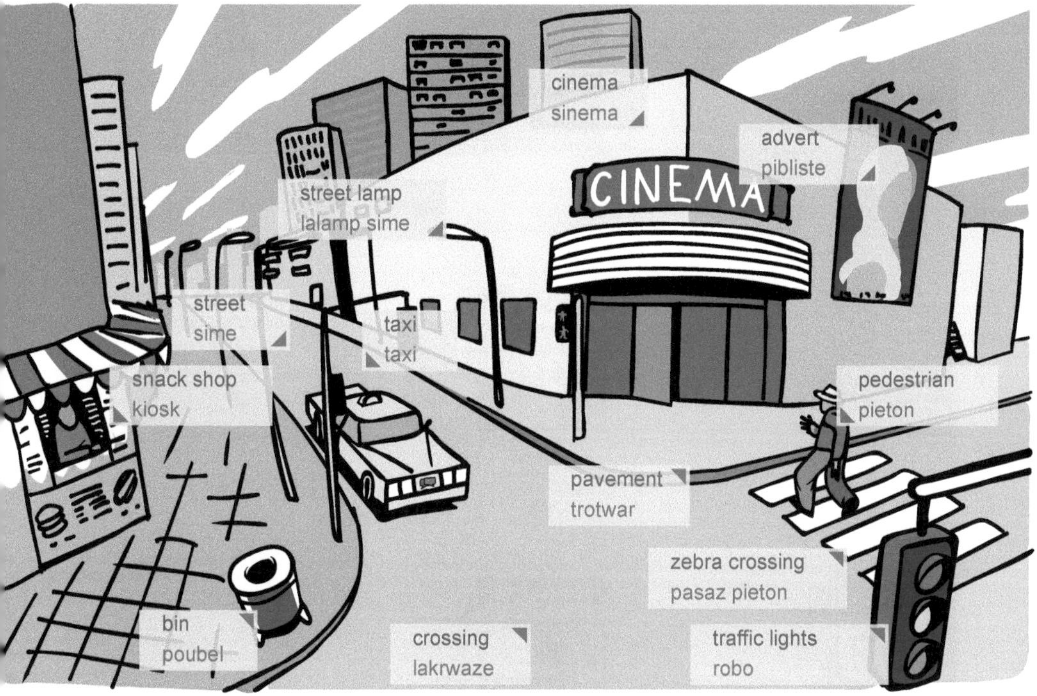

cinema
sinema

advert
pibliste

street lamp
lalamp sime

CINEMA

street
sime

taxi
taxi

snack shop
kiosk

pedestrian
pieton

pavement
trotwar

zebra crossing
pasaz pieton

bin
poubel

crossing
lakrwaze

traffic lights
robo

hut
kabann

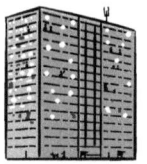

flat
flat

train station
stasion trin

town hall
minisipalite

museum
mize

school
lekol

university

liniversite

bank

labank

hospital

lopital

hotel

lotel

pharmacy

farmasi

office

biro

book shop

libreri

shop

magazin

florist's

fleris

supermarket

sipermarse

market

bazar

department store

gran magazin

fishmonger's

pwasonnri

shopping centre

sant komersial

harbour

lepor

park

park

bench

labank

bridge

pon

stairs

leskalie

underground

metro

tunnel

tinel

bus stop

bistop

bar

bar

restaurant

restoran

postbox

bwat-a-let

street sign

pano

parking meter

parkmet

zoo

zoo

swimming pool

pisinn

mosque

moske

farm

laferm

pollution

polision

graveyard

simitier

church

legliz

playground

lespas pou zwe

temple

tanp

# landscape

## peizaz

signpost
pano indikasion

way
sime

meadow
preri

stone
ros

tree
pie

hiker
randonner

river
larivier

grass
lerb

flower
fler

valley

lavale

hill

kolinn

lake

lak

forest

bwa

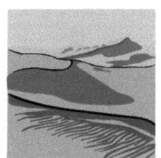

desert

dezer

volcano

volkan

castle

sato

rainbow

larkansiel

mushroom

sanpinion

palm tree

palmie

mosquito

moutik

fly

mous

ant

fourmi

bee

abey

spider

zarenie

beetle

koksinel

frog

grenouy

squirrel

ekirey

hedgehog

erison

hare

lapin

owl

ibou

bird

zwazo

swan

sign

boar

sangliye

deer

serf

moose

elan

dam

dam

wind turbine

eolienn

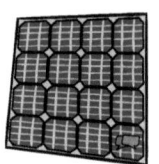

solar panel

pano soler

climate

klima

# restaurant
## restoran

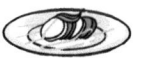

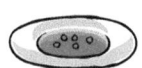

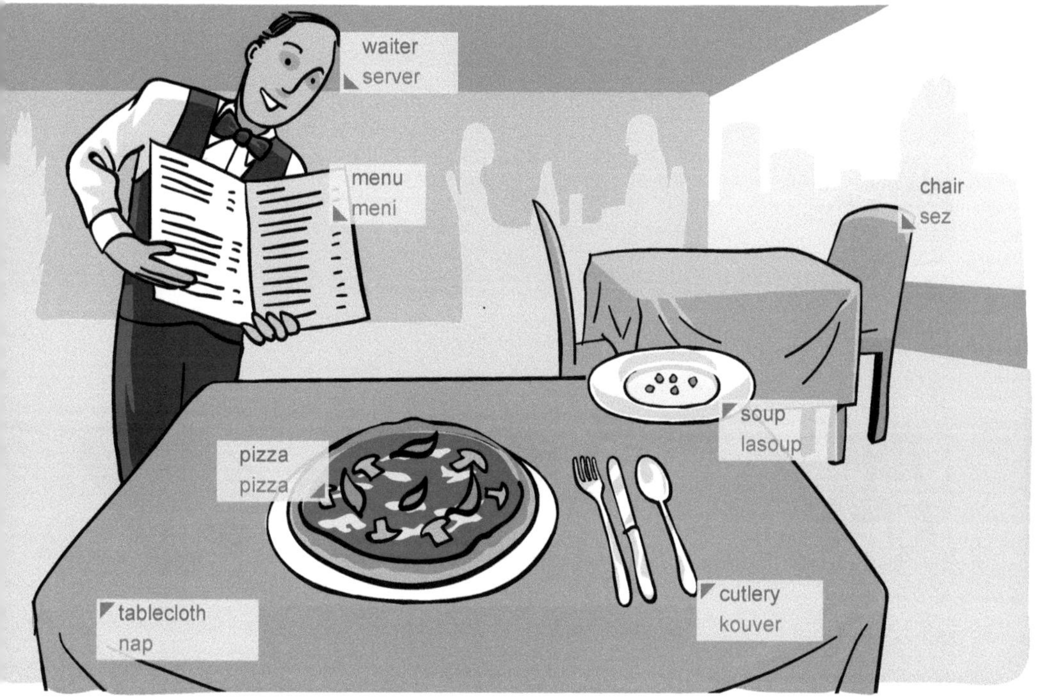
waiter
server
menu
meni
chair
sez
soup
lasoup
pizza
pizza
cutlery
kouver
tablecloth
nap

starter
lantre

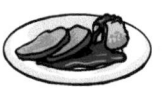

main course
pla prinsipal

dessert
deser

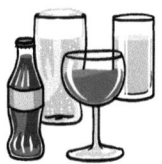

drinks
labwason

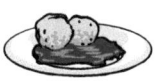

food
manze

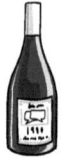

bottle
boutey

fast food

fast food

street food

take-away

teapot

teyer

sugar bowl

po disik

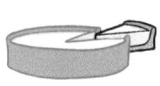

portion

porsion

espresso machine

masinn expresso

high chair

sez-ot

bill

bill

tray

plato

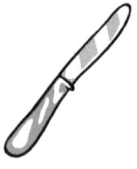

knife

kouto

fork

fourset

spoon

kwiyer

teaspoon

ti-kwiyer

serviette

serviet

glass

ver

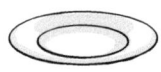

plate

lasiet

soup plate

lasiet

saucer

soukoup

sauce

lasos

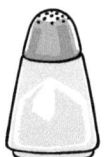

salt pot

po disel

pepper mill

moulin dipwav

vinegar

vineg

oil

delwil

spices

zepis

ketchup

ketchup

mustard

lamoutard

mayonnaise

mayonez

# supermarket

## sipermarse

special offer
promosion
FOR
customer
klian
dairy
prodwi a baz dile
trolley
trole
fruit
frwi

BUTCHERS

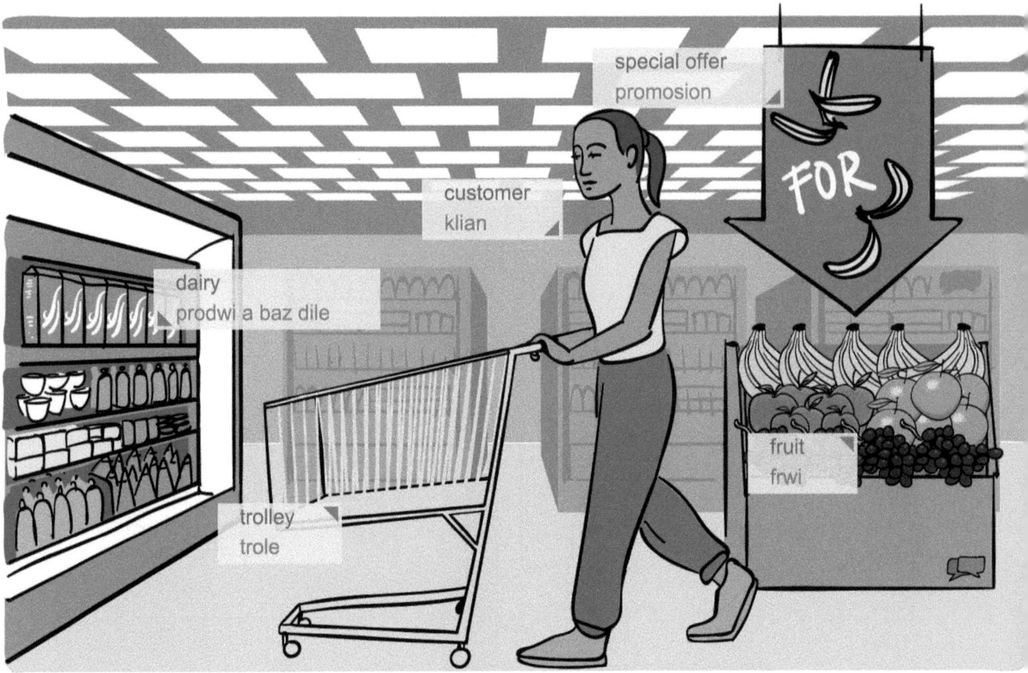

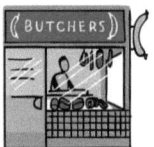

butcher´s

bousri

BAKERY

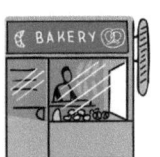

baker´s

boulanzri

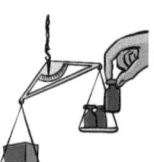

weigh

peze

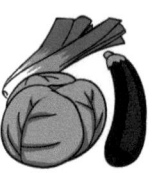

vegetables

legim

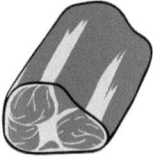

meat

laviann

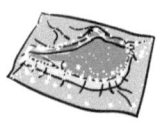

frozen food

aliman konzele

**cold meat**
sarkitri

**tinned food**
bwat konserv

**washing powder**
lapoud masinn

**sweets**
bonbon

**household products**
komision

**cleaning products**
deterzan

**salesperson**
vandez

**till**
lakes

**cashier**
kesie

**shopping list**
lalis komision

**opening hours**
ouvertir

**wallet**
portfey

**credit card**
kart kredi

**bag**
sak

**plastic bag**
sak plastik

# drinks

## labwason

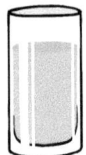

water

delo

juice

zi

milk

dile

coke

coca

wine

divin

beer

labier

alcohol

lalkol

cocoa

sokola so

tea

dite

coffee

kafe

espresso

expresso

cappuccino

cappuccino

banana

banann

apple

pom

orange

zoranz

melon

melon

lemon

sitron

carrot

karot

garlic

lay

bamboo

banbou

onion

zwayon

mushroom

sanpiyon

nuts

nwazet

noodles

minn

spaghetti

spageti

rice

diri

salad

salad

chips

chips

fried potatoes

pomdeter frir

pizza

pizza

hamburger

burger

sandwich

sandwich

cutlet

eskalop

ham

zanbon

salami

salami

sausage

sosis

chicken

poul

roast

roti

fish

pwason

porridge oats

oatmeal

muesli

muesli

cornflakes

kornbif

flour

lafarinn

croissant

krwasan

bread roll

ti-dipin

bread

dipin

toast

dipin griye

biscuits

biskwi

butter

diber

curd

fromaz blan

cake

gato

egg

dizef

fried egg

dizef frir

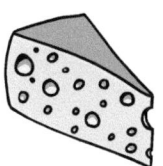

cheese

fromaz

ice cream

sorbe

sugar

disik

honey

dimiel

jam

konfitir

chocolate spread

nouga

curry

kari

# farm
# laferm

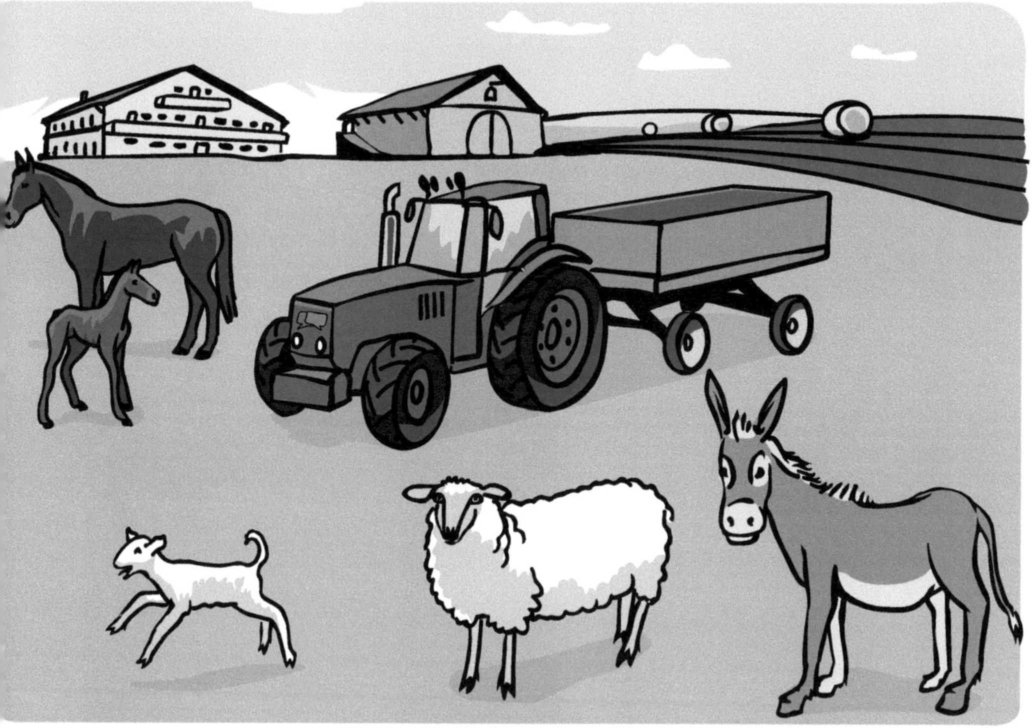

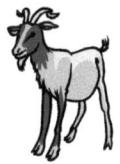

goat

kabri

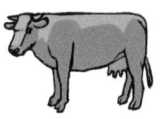

cow

vas

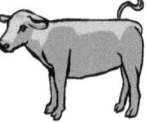

calf

vo

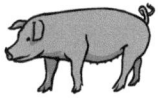

pig

koson

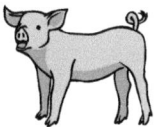

piglet

ti-koson

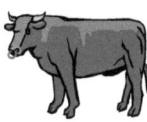

bull

toro

goose

lezwa

duck

kanar

chick

pousin

hen

poul

cock

kok

rat

lera

cat

sat

mouse

souri

ox

bef

dog

lisien

doghouse

lakaz lisien

garden hose

tiyo

watering can

arozwar

scythe

laserp

plough

saret

sickle

fosi

hoe

pios

pitchfork

fours

axe

lars

wheelbarrow

bouret

trough

kiv

milk can

bwat dile

sack

sak

fence

fencing

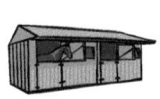

stable

letab

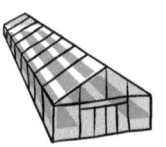

greenhouse

laser

soil

later

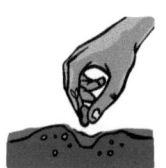

seed

lagrin

fertilizer

langre

combine harvester

masinn pou fer rekolt

harvest

rekolte

harvest

rekolt

yams

ignam

wheat

dible

soy

soya

potato

pomdeter

corn

may

rapeseed

colza

fruit tree

zarb frwitie

cassava

maniok

cereals

sereal

living room
salon

bathroom
saldebin

kitchen
lakwizinn

bedroom
lasam

child's room
lasam zanfan

dining room
salamanze

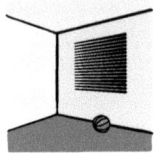

floor

sali

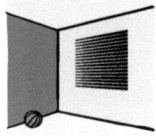

wall

miray

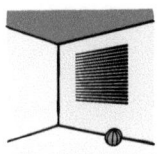

ceiling

plafon

cellar

lakav

sauna

sona

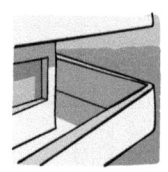

balcony

balkon

terrace

teras

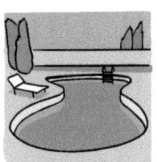

pool

pisinn

lawn mower

masinn koup gazon

sheet

dra

bedspread

kwet

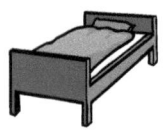

bed

lili

broom

balie

bucket

seo

switch

take lalimier

carpet
tapi

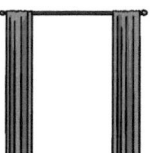

curtain
rido

table
latab

chair
sez

rocking chair
rocking chair

armchair
fotey

book
liv

blanket
kouvertir

decoration
dekorasion

firewood
dibwa foye

film
fim

hi-fi equipment
hi-fi

key
lakle

newspaper
zournal

painting
lapintir

poster
poster

radio
radio

notepad
bloknot

hoover
laspirater

cactus
kaktis

candle
labouzi

# kitchen
# lakwizinn

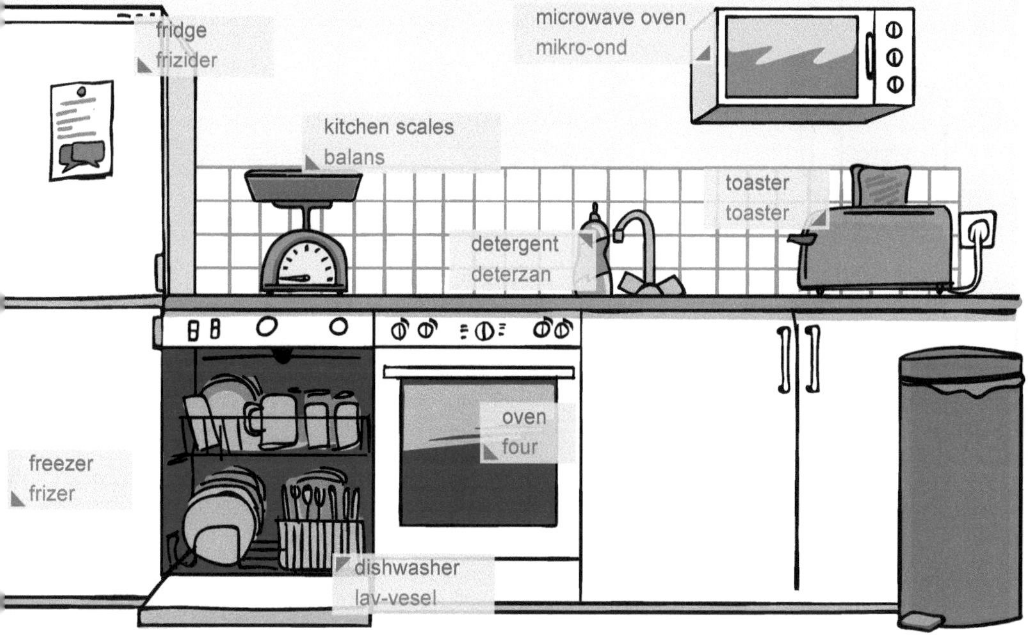

fridge
frizider
microwave oven
mikro-ond
kitchen scales
balans
toaster
toaster
detergent
deterzan
oven
four
freezer
frizer
dishwasher
lav-vesel


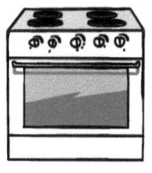

cooker
four

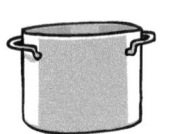

pot
kasrol

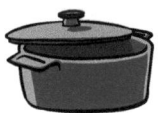

cast-iron pot
marmit

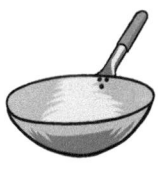

wok / kadai
wok

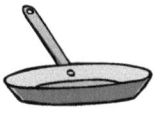

pan
pwal

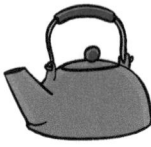

kettle
boulwar

steamer
steamer

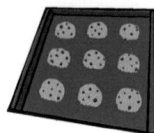

baking tray
plak kwison

crockery
vesel

mug
goble

bowl
bol

chopsticks
baget sinwa

ladle
lous

spatula
spatil

whisk
fwet

strainer
paswar

sieve
tami

grater
larap

mortar
mortie

barbecue
griyad

open fire
lasemine

chopping board

biyo

rolling pin

roulo

corkscrew

tirbouson

can

bwat konserv

can opener

ouvbwat

pot holder

legan proteksion

sink

lavabo

brush

bros

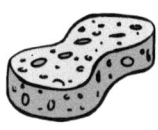

sponge

leponz

blender

blender

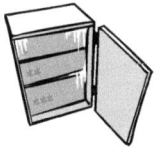

deep freezer

konzelater

baby bottle

bibron

tap

robine

# bathroom
## saldebin

shower
dous

heating
sofaz

towel
serviet

shower curtain
rido dous

bubble bath
bin mousan

bathtub
benwar

glass
ver

washing machine
masinn lave

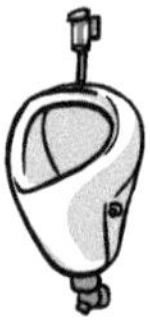

tap
robine

tiles
karo

potty
potsam

sink
lavabo

| | | |
|---|---|---|
| toilet | squat toilet | bidet |
| twalet | twalet | bide |
| urinal | toilet paper | toilet brush |
| piswar | papie twalet | bros twalet |

**toothbrush**

bros ledan

**toothpaste**

dantifris

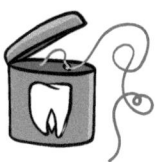

**dental floss**

fil danter

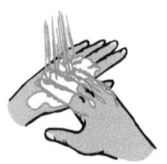

**wash**

lave

**handheld shower**

ti-bin

**douche**

dous

**basin**

basin

**back brush**

bros ledo

**soap**

savon

**shower gel**

zel dous

**shampoo**

sanpwin

**flannel**

gandebin

**drain**

drin

**cream**

lakrem

**deodorant**

deodoran

mirror

mirwar

hand mirror

mirwar

razor

razwar

shaving foam

lamous pou raze

aftershave

apre-razaz

comb

pengn

brush

bros

hair dryer

seswar

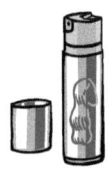

hairspray

lak

makeup

makiyaz

lipstick

dirouz

nail varnish

verni

cotton wool

cotton wool

nail scissors

tay-zong

perfume

parfin

washbag

trous twalet

stool

stoul

weighing scale

balans

bathrobe

penwar

rubber gloves

legan netwayaz

tampon

tanpon

sanitary towel

serviet izienik

chemical toilet

twalet simik

# child's room
# lasam zanfan

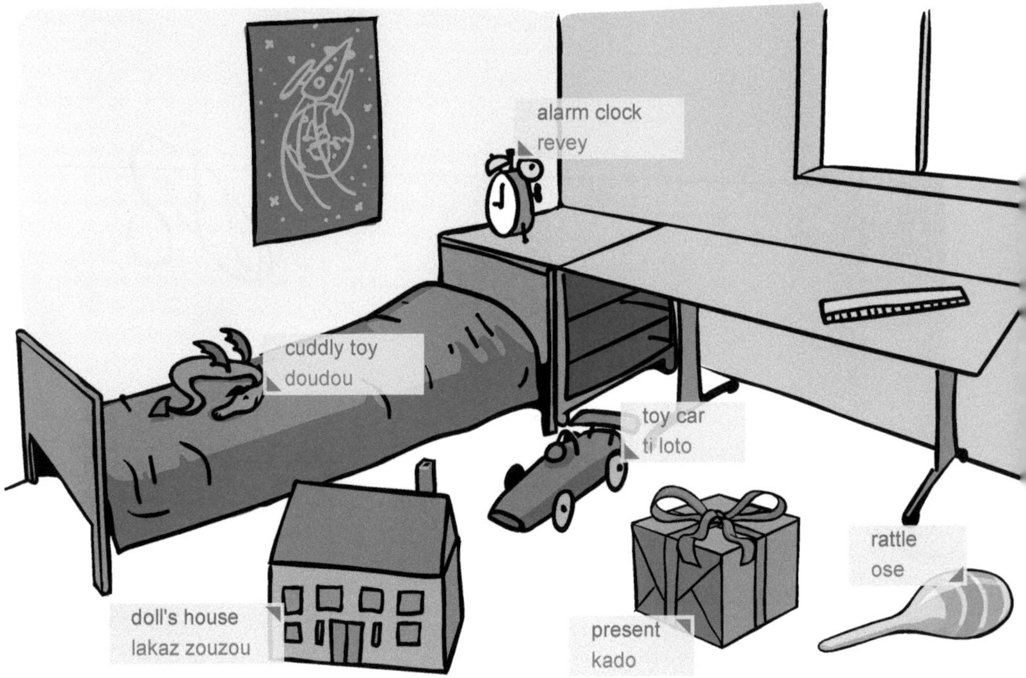
alarm clock
revey
cuddly toy
doudou
toy car
ti loto
rattle
ose
doll's house
lakaz zouzou
present
kado

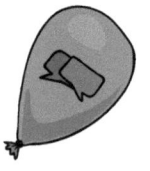

balloon
balon

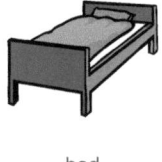

bed
lili

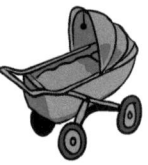

pram
pouset

deck of cards
kart

jigsaw
puzzle

SUPER
MEGA

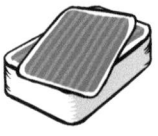

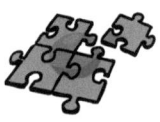

comic
tikomik

lego bricks

lego

building blocks

lego

action figure

figirinn

babygrow

grenouyer

frisbee

frisbee

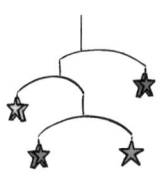

mobile

mobil

board game

zwe

dice

lede

model train set

trin zouzou

dummy

siset

party

fet

picture book

liv ek zimaz

ball

boul

doll

poupet

play

zwe

sandpit

bak-a-sab

swing

balanswar

toys

zouzou

video game console

game

tricycle

trisik

teddy bear

nounours

wardrobe

larmwar

## clothing
## linz

socks

soset

stockings

leba

tights

kolan

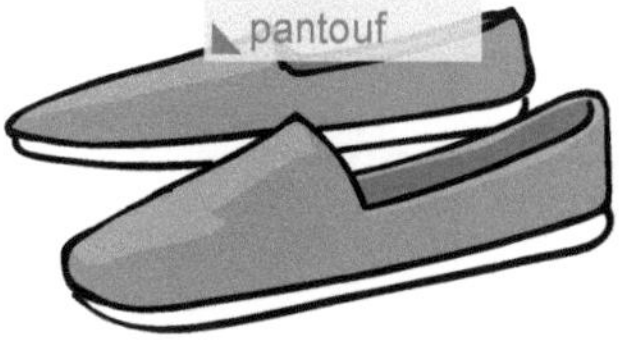

scarf
esarp

umbrella
parapli

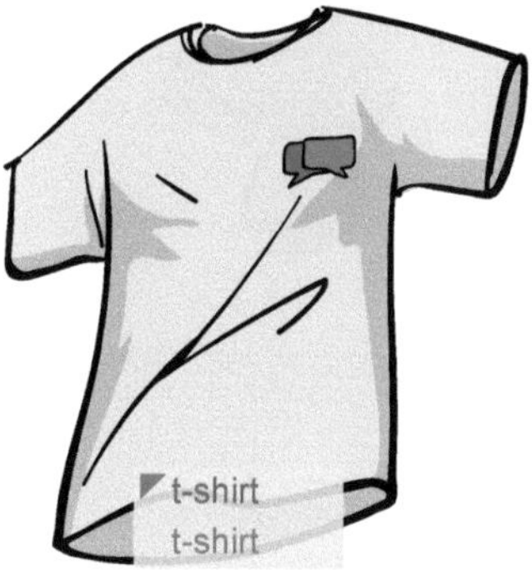

t-shirt
t-shirt

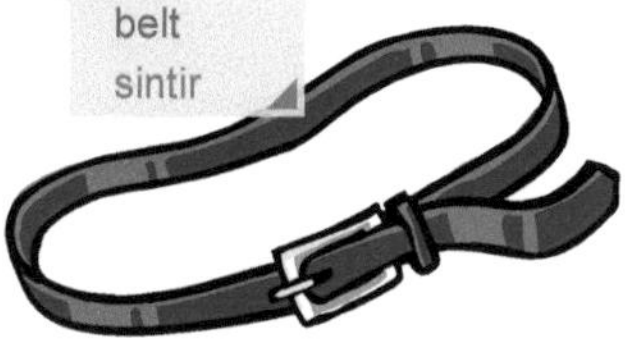

belt
sintir

boots
bot

slippers
pantouf

trainers
tenis

sandals
.................
sandalet

shoes
.................
soulie

rubber boots
.................
bot an karotsou

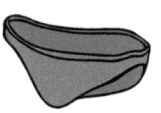

underpants
.................
souvetman

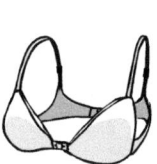

bra
.................
soutiengorz

vest
.................
vest

body
body

trousers
pantalon

jeans
jeans

skirt
zip

blouse
blouz

shirt
simiz

pullover
pull-over

hoodie
blouzon ek kapison

blazer
vest

jacket
jaket

coat
manto

raincoat
pardesi

costume
kostim

dress
rob

wedding dress
rob lamarye

suit

kostim

nightgown

robdesam

pyjamas

pizama

sari

sari

headscarf

foular

turban

tirban

burqa

bourka

kaftan

kaftan

abaya

abaya

swimsuit

mayo de bin

trunks

mayo de bin

shorts

sorti de sekour

tracksuit

linz spor

apron

tabliye

gloves

legan

button
bouton

glasses
linet

bracelet
brasle

necklace
kolie

ring
bag

earring
zanon

cap
bone

coat hanger
sint

hat
sapo

tie
kravat

zip
fermetirekler

helmet
elmet

braces
bretel

school uniform
iniform lekol

uniform
iniform

bib

bavwar

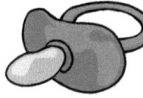

dummy

siset

nappy

lanz

server
server

filing cabinet
larmwar arsiv

printer
printer

paper
papie

monitor
lekran

desk
biro

mouse
mouse

folder
klaser

keyboard
klavie

waste-paper basket
poubel

chair
sez

computer
ordinater

coffee mug

mug

calculator

kalkilatris

internet

internet

office - biro

49

laptop
laptop

letter
let

message
mesaz

mobile
portab

network
rezo

photocopier
fotokopi

software
lozisiel

telephone
telefonn

plug socket
priz

fax machine
fax

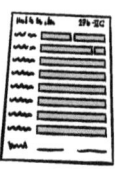

form
form

document
dokiman

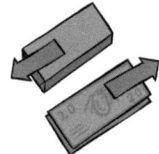

buy
aste

pay
peye

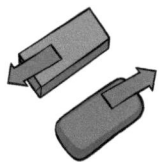

trade
fer biznes

money
larzan

dollar
dolar

euro
euro

yen
yen

rouble
rouble

Swiss franc
fran swis

renminbi yuan
renminbi yuan

rupee
roupi

cashpoint
distribiter biye

bureau de change

biro sanz

gold

lor

silver

larzan

oil

petrol

energy

lenerzi

price

pri

contract

kontra

tax

tax

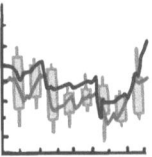

stock

aksion

work

travay

employee

anplwaye

employer

anplwayer

factory

lizinn

shop

magazin

police officer
polisie

fireman
ponpie

cook
kwizinie

doctor
dokter

pilot
pilot

gardener

zardinie

carpenter

sarpantie

seamstress

koutirier

judge

ziz

chemist

simis

actor

akter

bus driver

sofer bis

taxi driver

sofer taxi

fisherman

peser

cleaning lady

bonn

roofer

zouvriye twa lakaz

waiter

server

hunter

saser

painter

pint

baker

boulanze

electrician

elektrisien

builder

zouvriye

engineer

inzenier

butcher

bouse

plumber

plonbie

postman

fakter

occupations - travay

soldier

solda

architect

arsitek

cashier

kesie

florist

fleris

hairdresser

kwafez

conductor

chek

mechanic

mekanisien

captain

kapitenn

dentist

dantis

scientist

siantis

rabbi

rabi

imam

imam

monk

mwann

clergyman

pret

occupations - travay

# tools
# zouti

hammer
marto
pliers
pins
screwdriver
tournavis
spanner
lakle
torch
tors


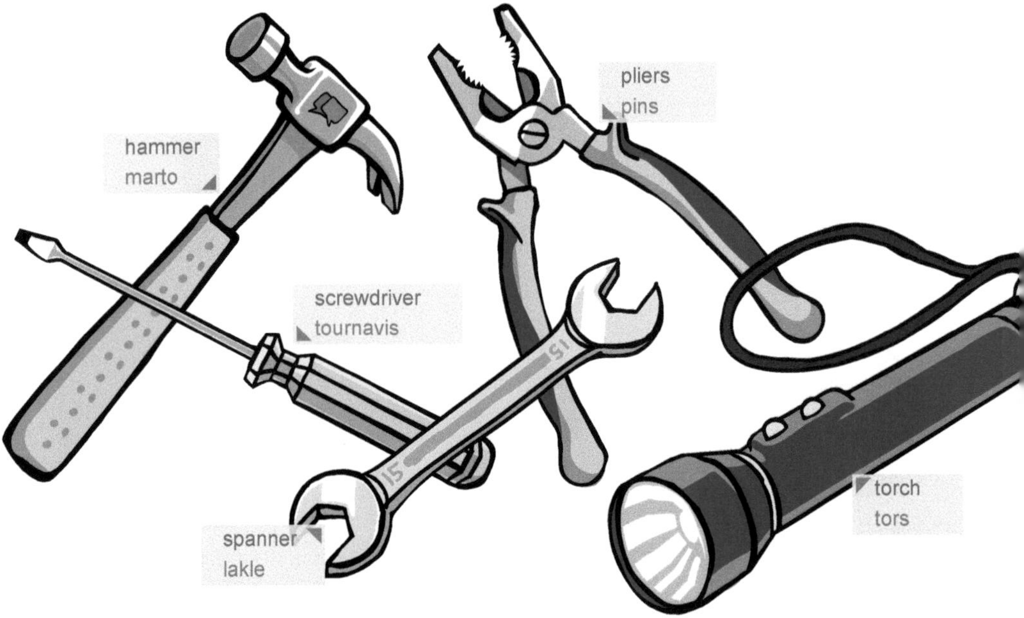

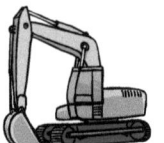

digger

peltez

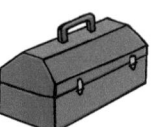

toolbox

bwat zouti

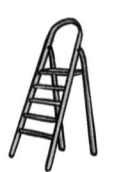

ladder

lesel

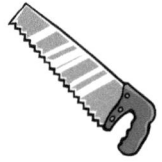

saw

lasi

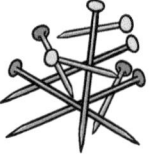

nails

koulou

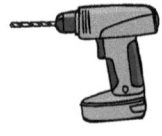

drill

persez

repair

aranze

shovel

lapel

Damn!

Ayo!

dustpan

lapel

paint pot

po lapintir

screws

vis

## musical instruments
## instriman lamizik

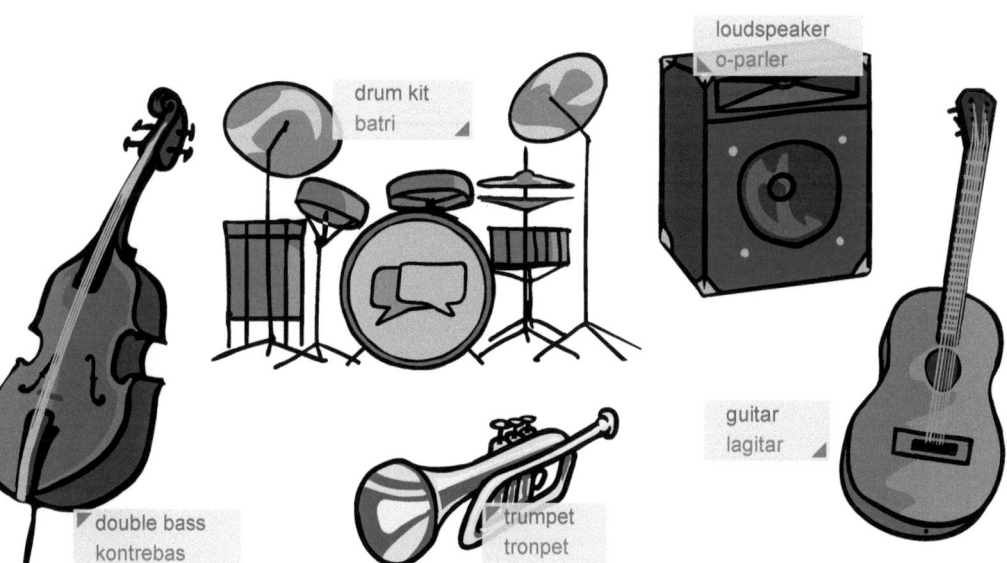

loudspeaker
o-parler

drum kit
batri

guitar
lagitar

double bass
kontrebas

trumpet
tronpet

piano

piano

violin

violon

bass

bas

timpani

tinbal

drums

tanbour

keyboard

klavie

saxophone

saxofonn

flute

laflit

microphone

mikro

# ZOO

# ZOO

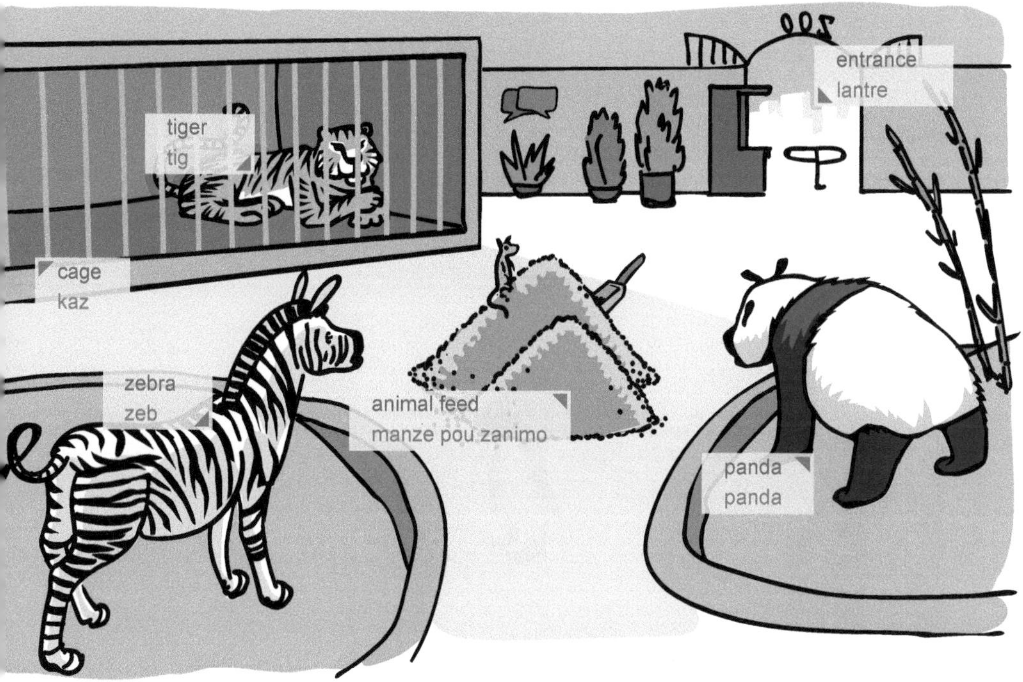
tiger
tig
entrance
lantre
cage
kaz
zebra
zeb
animal feed
manze pou zanimo
panda
panda

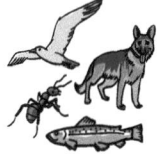

animals

zanimo

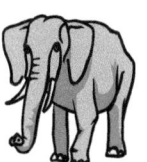

elephant

lelefan

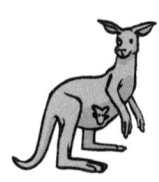

kangaroo

kangourou

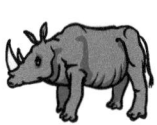

rhino

rinoceros

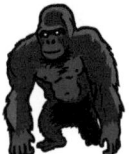

gorilla

gori

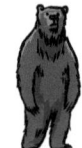

bear

lours

camel

samo

ostrich

lotris

lion

lion

monkey

zako

flamingo

flaman roz

parrot

peroke

polar bear

lours poler

penguin

pingwi

shark

rekin

peacock

pan

snake

serpan

crocodile

krokodil

zookeeper

gardien zoo

seal

fok

jaguar

zagwar

pony

poney

leopard

leopar

hippo

ipopotam

giraffe

ziraf

eagle

leg

boar

sangliye

fish

pwason

turtle

torti

walrus

mors

fox

renar

gazelle

gazel

American football
foutborl ameriken

cycling
siklism

tennis
tenis

basketball
basketball

swimming
natasion

boxing
labox

ice hockey
oke lor gazon

football
foutborl

badminton
badminton

athletics
atletism

handball
handball

skiing
ski

polo
polo

# activities
# aktivite

laugh
riye
jump
sote
hug
maye
walk
marse
sing
sante
dream
reve
pray
priye
kiss
anbrase

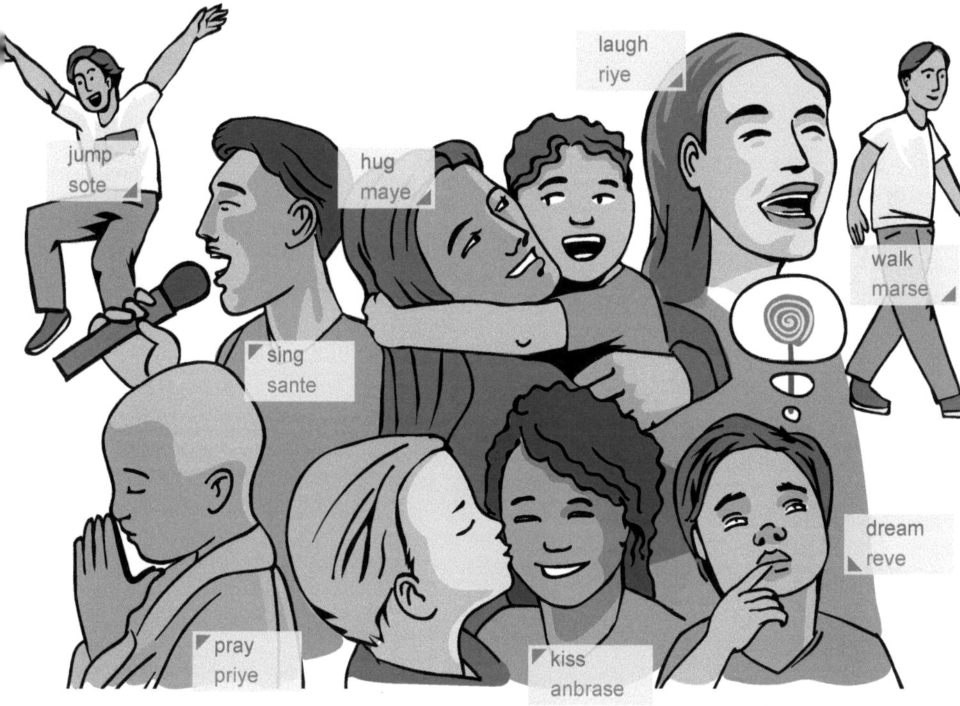

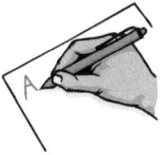

write

ekrir

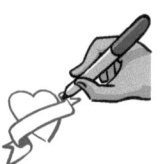

draw

desine

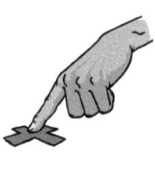

show

montre

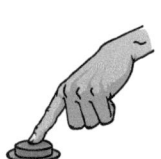

push

pouse

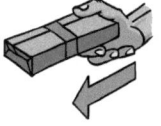

give

done

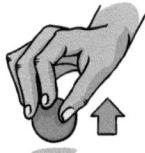

take

pran

have

ena

do

fer

be

ete

stand

diboute

run

galoupe

pull

rise

throw

zete

fall

tonbe

lie

alonze

wait

atann

carry

amene

sit

asize

get dressed

abiye

sleep

dormi

wake up

leve

look at
gete

cry
plore

stroke
karese

comb
pengne

talk
koze

understand
konpran

ask
dimande

listen
ekoute

drink
bwar

eat
manze

tidy up
netwaye

love
kontan

cook
kwi

drive
kondir

fly
anvole

sail

fer lavwal

calculate

kalkile

read

lir

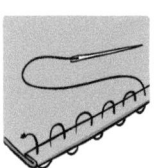

learn

aprann

work

travay

marry

marye

sew

koud

brush teeth

bros ledan

kill

touye

smoke

fime

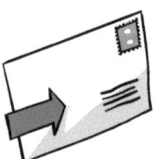

send

avoye

# family
# fami

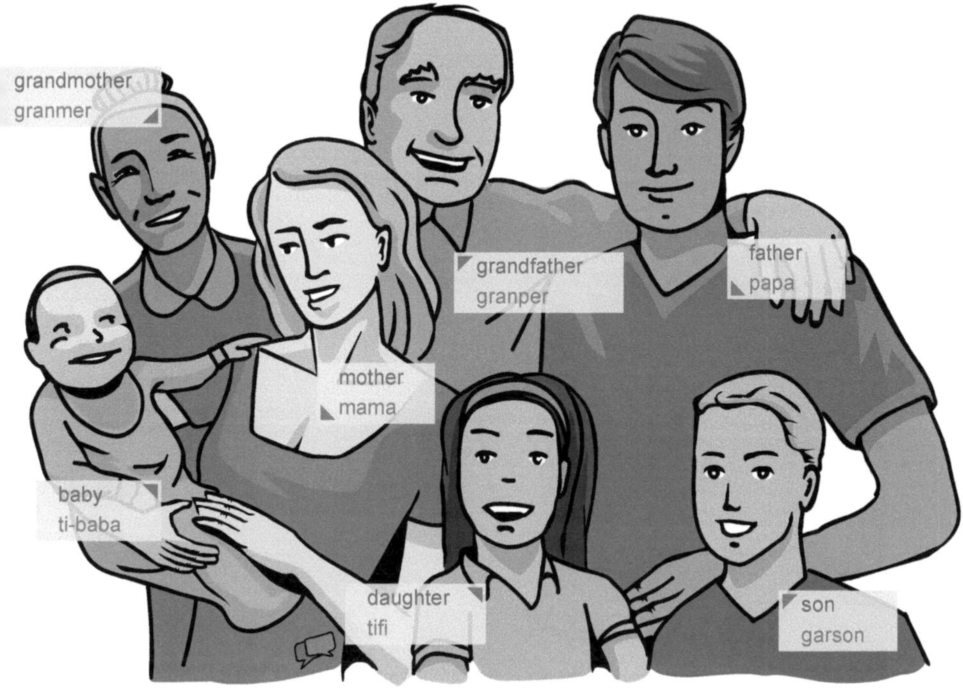
grandmother
granmer
grandfather
granper
father
papa
mother
mama
baby
ti-baba
daughter
tifi
son
garson

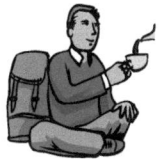

guest
ot

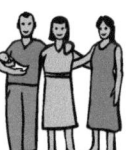

aunt
matant

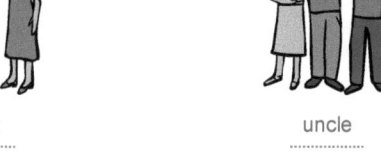

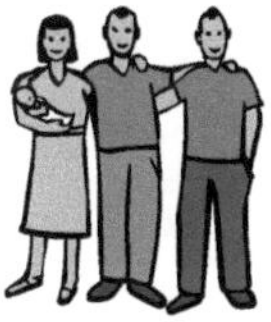

uncle
tonton

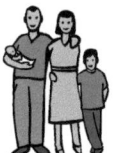

brother
frer

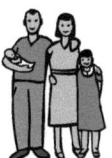

sister
ser

# body

## lekor

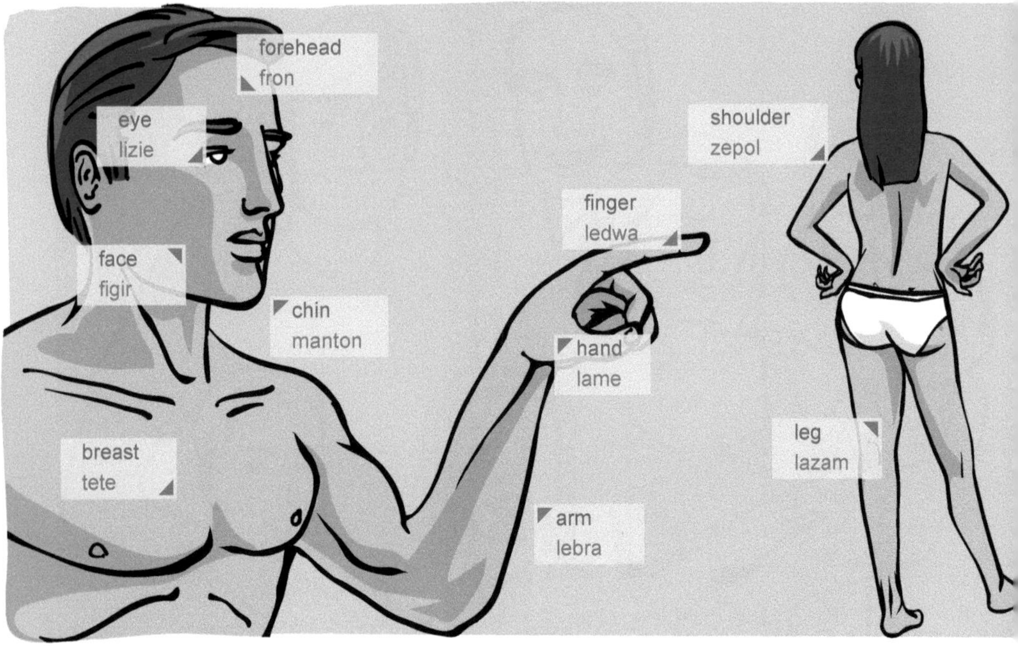

forehead
fron

eye
lizie

shoulder
zepol

finger
ledwa

face
figir

chin
manton

hand
lame

leg
lazam

breast
tete

arm
lebra

baby

ti-baba

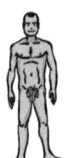

man

zom

woman

fam

girl

tifi

boy

ti-garson

head

latet

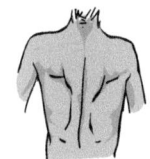

back

ledo

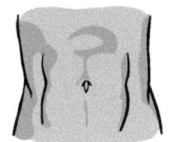

belly

vant

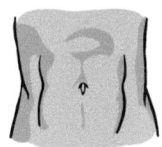

belly button

lonbri

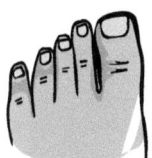

toe

zortey

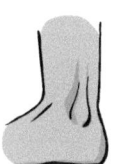

heel

talon

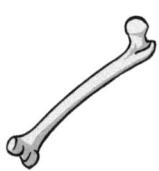

bone

lezo

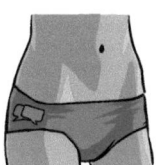

hip

laans

knee

zenou

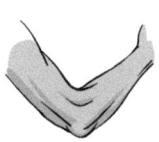

elbow

koud

nose

nene

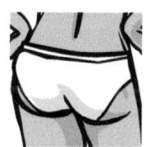

bottom

fes

skin

lapo

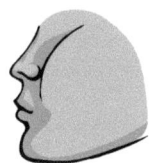

cheek

lazou

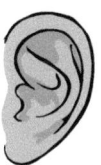

ear

zorey

lip

lalev

mouth

labous

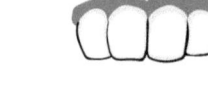

tooth

ledan

tongue

lalang

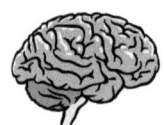

brain

servo

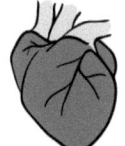

heart

leker

muscle

mix

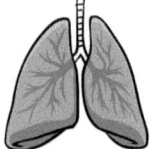

lung

poumon

liver

lefwa

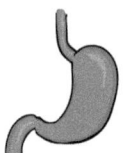

stomach

lestoma

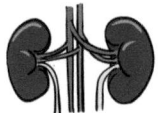

kidneys

lerin

sex

sex

condom

kapot

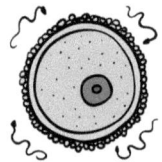

ovum

ovil

semen

sperm

pregnancy

groses

body - lekor

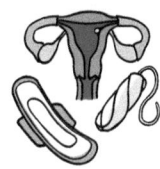

menstruation
period

vagina
vazin

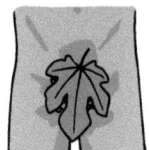

penis
penis

eyebrow
soursi

hair
seve

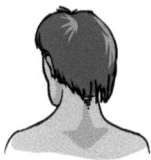

neck
likou

# hospital
# lopital

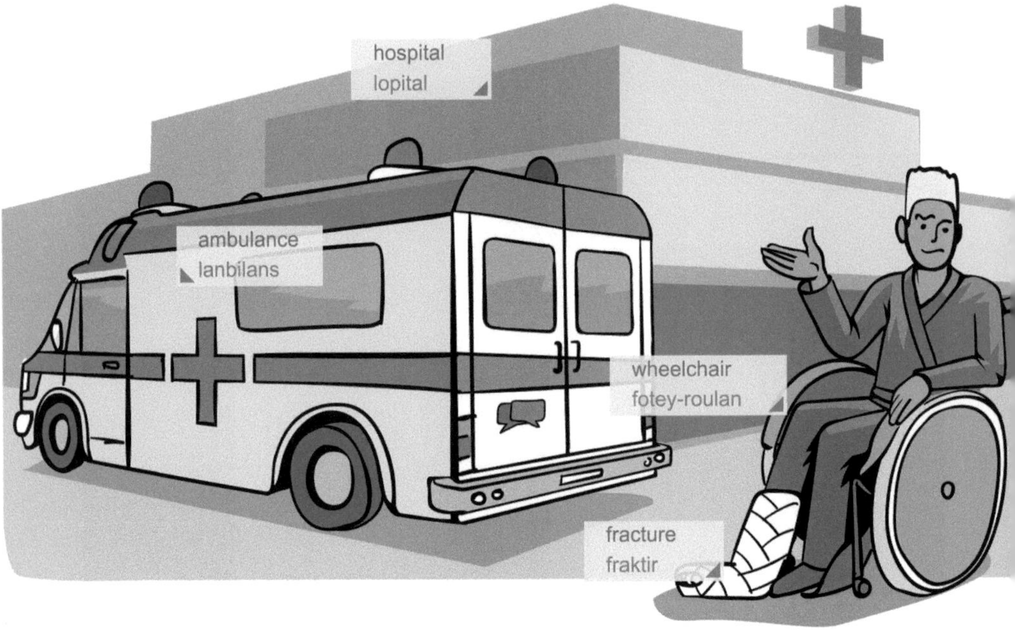

hospital
lopital
ambulance
lanbilans
wheelchair
fotey-roulan
fracture
fraktir

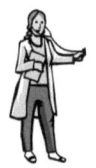

doctor
dokter

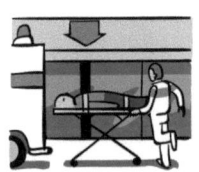

emergency room
servis irzans

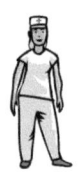

nurse
ners

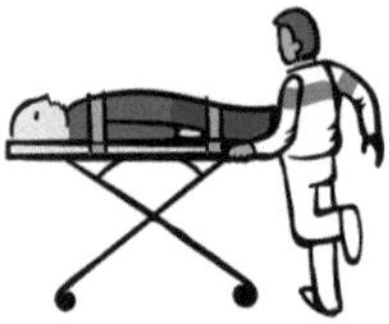

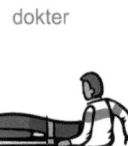

emergency
irzans

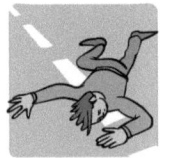

unconscious
inkonsian

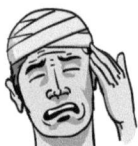

pain
douler

injury

blesir

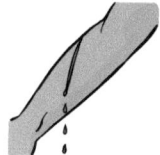

bleeding

emorazi

heart attack

kriz kardiak

stroke

atak serebral

allergy

alerzik

cough

touse

fever

lafiev

flu

lagrip

diarrhoea

diare

headache

malad latet

cancer

kanser

diabetes

diabet

surgeon

sirirzien

scalpel

skalpel

operation

operasion

CT

CT

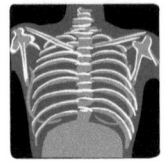

x-ray

x-ray

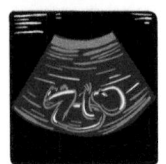

ultrasound

iltrason

face mask

mask

disease

maladi

waiting room

sal-datant

crutch

beki

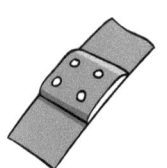

plaster

pansman

bandage

bandaz

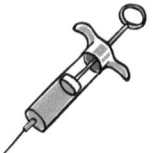

injection

inzeksion

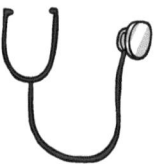

stethoscope

stetoskop

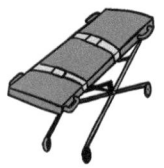

stretcher

brankar

clinical thermometer

termomet

birth

nesans

overweight

sirpwa

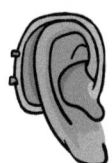

hearing aid
laparey oditif

disinfectant
dezinfektan

infection
infeksion

virus
viris

HIV / AIDS
HIV / SIDA

medicine
medsinn

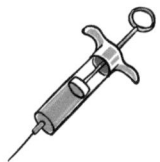

vaccination
vaksinasion

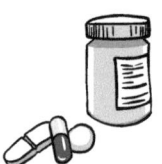

tablets
konprime

pill
pilil kontraseptif

emergency call
korl irzans

blood pressure monitor
laparey tansion

ill / healthy
malad / bien

| | | |
|---|---|---|
| Help! <br> o-sekour |  <br> alarm <br> alarm |  <br> assault <br> atak |
| 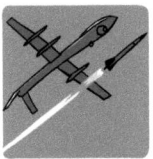 <br> attack <br> atak |  <br> danger <br> danze |  <br> emergency exit <br> sorti de sekour |
| Fire! <br> Dife! |  <br> fire extinguisher <br> laponp dife |  <br> accident <br> aksidan |
| 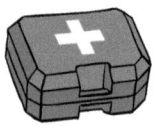 <br> first-aid kit <br> kit first aid |  <br> SOS <br> SOS |  <br> police <br> lapolis |

Europe

Ierop

North America

Lamerik di nor

South America

Lamerik di sid

Africa

Iafrik

Asia

Iazi

Australia

Iostrali

Atlantic

Iatlantik

Pacific

pasifik

Indian Ocean

Iosean indien

Antarctic Ocean

Iosean antartik

Arctic Ocean

Iosean artik

North Pole

Pol Nor

South Pole

Pol Sid

Antarctica

lantartik

Earth

later

land

later

sea

lamer

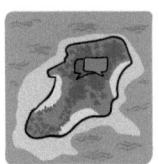

island

zil

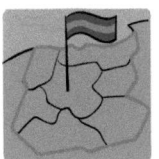

nation

nasion

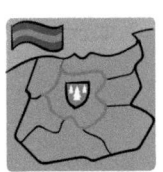

state

leta

clock face

kadran

hour hand

zegwi ler

minute hand

zegwi minit

second hand

zegwi segonn

What time is it?

ki ler la ?

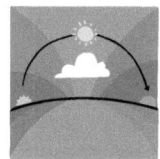

day

zour

time

letan

now

aster-la

digital watch

mont dizital

minute

minit

hour

ler

# week

## lasemenn

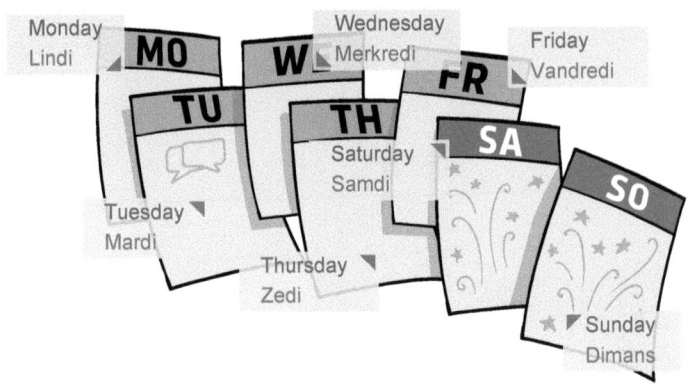

| | | |
|---|---|---|
| Monday Lindi | Wednesday Merkredi | Friday Vandredi |
| Tuesday Mardi | Thursday Zedi | Saturday Samdi |
| | | Sunday Dimans |

yesterday

yer

today

zordi

tomorrow

demin

morning

gramatin

noon

midi

evening

aswar

business days

zour travay

weekend

wikenn

# year
## lane

rain
lapli
spring
printan
summer
lete
wind
divan[
autumn
otonn
snow
lanez
winter
liver


4.APRIL 11°
5.APRIL 4°
6.APRIL 13°
7.APRIL 8°
8.APRIL 10°


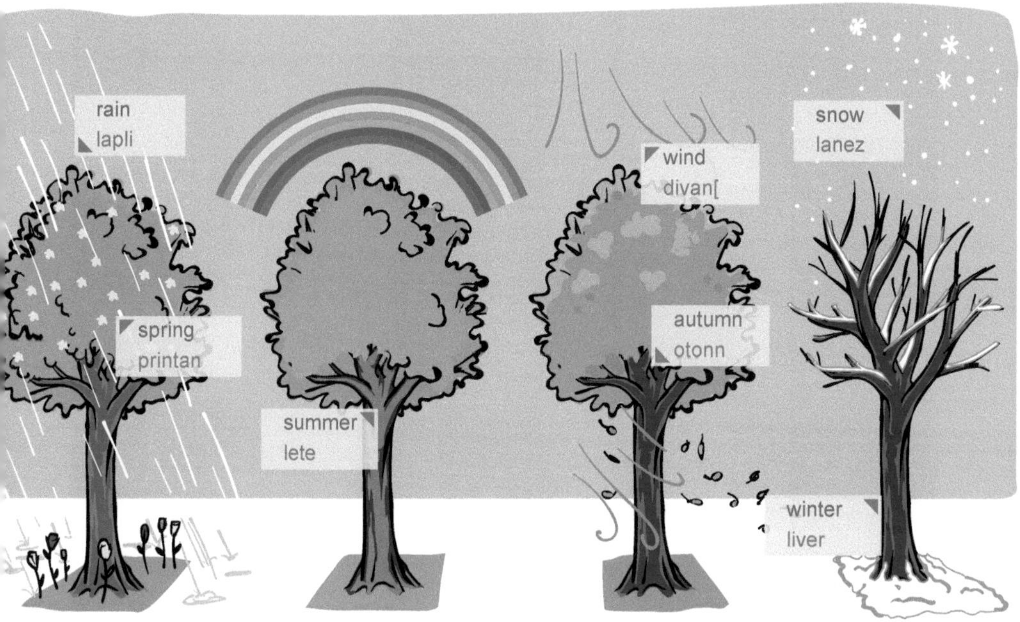

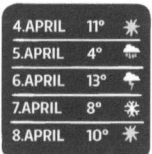

weather forecast

meteo

F C
120 90 60 30 0 -30
40 30 20 10 0 -10 -20


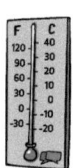

thermometer

termomet

sunshine

lalimier soley

cloud

niaz

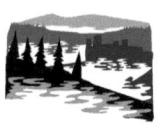

fog

brouyar

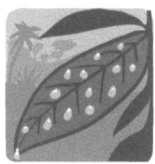

humidity

limidite

lightning

lafoud

thunder

toner

storm

tanpet

hail

lagrel

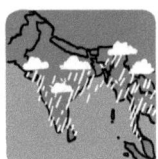

monsoon

mouson

flood

inondasion

ice

laglas

January

Zanvie

February

Fevriye

March

Mars

April

Avril

May

Me

June

Zien

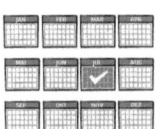

July

Zilie

August

Out

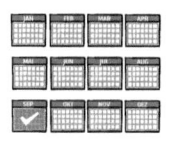

September
...............
Septam

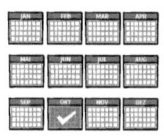

October
...............
Oktob

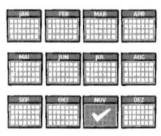

November
...............
Novam

December
...............
Desam

# shapes
## form

circle
...............
ron

square
...............
kare

rectangle
...............
rektang

triangle
...............
triang

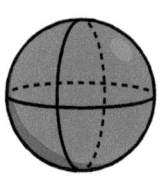

sphere
...............
sfer

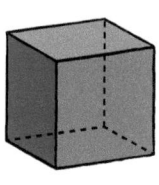

cube
...............
kib

white

blan

yellow

zonn

orange

oranz

pink

roz

red

rouz

purple

mov

blue

ble

green

ver

brown

maron

grey

gri

black

nwar

a lot / a little

boukou / enn tigit

angry / calm

ankoler / kalm

beautiful / ugly

zoli / vilin

beginning / end

koumansman / lafin

big / small

gro / tipti

bright / dark

kler / obskirite

brother / sister

frer / ser

clean / dirty

prop / sal

complete / incomplete

konple / inkonple

day / night

lizour / lanwit

dead / alive

vivan / mor

wide / narrow

larz / sere

edible / inedible

komestib / inkomestib

evil / kind

move / bon

excited / bored

exsite / agase

fat / thin

gra / mins

first / last

premie / dernie

friend / enemy

kamwad / lennmi

full / empty

ranpli / vid

hard / soft

dir / mou

heavy / light

lour / leze

hunger / thirst

fin / swaf

ill / healthy

malad / bien

illegal / legal

ilegal / legal

intelligent / stupid

intelizan / kouyon

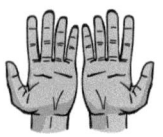

left / right

gos / drwat

near / far

pre / lwin

new / used
nouvo / ize

nothing / something
nanye / kiksoz

old / young
vie / zenn

on / off
demare / arete

open / closed
ouver / ferme

quiet / loud
trankil / for

rich / poor
ris / pov

right / wrong
bon / move

rough / smooth
brit / lis

sad / happy
tris / zwaye

short / long
kourt / long

slow / fast
lan / rapid

wet / dry
tranpe / sek

warm / cool
so / fre

war / peace
lager / lape

**0**

zero

zero

**1**

one

enn

**2**

two

de

**3**

three

trwa

**4**

four

kat

**5**

five

sink

**6**

six

sis

**7**

seven

set

**8**

eight

wit

**9**

nine

nef

**10**

ten

distribiter biye

**11**

eleven

onz

**12**

twelve

douz

**13**

thirteen

trez

**14**

fourteen

katorz

**15**

fifteen

kinz

**16**

sixteen

sez

**17**

seventeen

diset

**18**

eighteen

dizwit

**19**

nineteen

diznef

**20**

twenty

vin

**100**

hundred

san

**1.000**

thousand

mil

**1.000.000**

million

milyon

English

Angle

American English

Angle Lamerik

Chinese Mandarin

Mandarin Sinwa

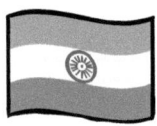

Hindi

Hindi

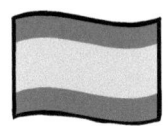

Spanish

espagnol

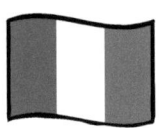

French

Franse

Arabic

Arab

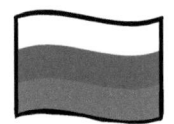

Russian

Ris

Portuguese

Portige

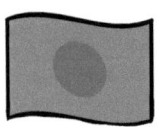

Bengali

Bengali

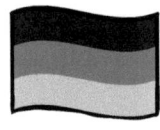

German

Alman

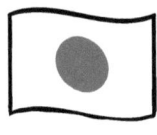

Japanese

Zapone

I
.................
mo

you
.................
to

he / she / it
.................
li

we
.................
nou

you
.................
ou

they
.................
zot

who?
.................
kisana?

what?
.................
kiete?

how?
.................
kouma?

where?
.................
kotsa?

when?
.................
kan?

name
.................
nom

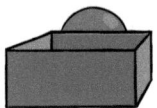

behind

deryer

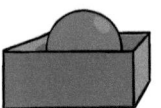

in

dan

in front of

devan

over

lor

on

lor

under

anba

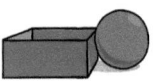

beside

akote

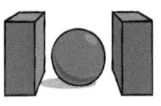

between

ant

place

plas